Greater Than a Tourist - Bucharest Romania

D1722012

50 Travel Tips from a Local

Cristina Tărbuc

Lock Haven, PA
All rights reserved.
ISBN: 9781521785232

> TOURIST

Cristina Tărbuc

BOOK DESCRIPTION

Are you excited about planning your next trip? Do you want to try
something new while traveling? Would you like some guidance
from a local? If you answered yes to any of these questions, then
this book is just for you.

Greater Than a Tourist - Bucharest, Romania by Cristina Tărbuc
offers the inside scope on Bucharest. Most travel books tell you
how to travel like a tourist. Although there's nothing wrong with
that, as a part of the Greater than a Tourist series, this book will
give you travel tips from someone who lives at your next travel
destination.

In these pages you'll discover local advice that will help you
throughout your stay. This book will not tell you exact addresses or
store hours but instead will give you an excitement and knowledge
from a local that you may not find in other smaller print travel
books. Travel like a local. Slow down, stay in one place, and get
to know the people and the culture of a place.

By the time you finish this book, you will be eager and prepared to
travel to your next destination.

TABLE OF CONTENTS

DEDICATION

This book is dedicated to my family and friends, even though they have no idea that I'm writing a book, or that it will get published.

Cristina Tărbuc

ABOUT THE AUTHOR

Cristina Tărbuc was born in a small Romanian town that didn't quite offer a lot of possibilities for a decent life, so after graduating from college in 2006, she decided to move to the capital, in pursue of fame and fortune.

As a newcomer in Bucharest, Cristina had to adapt and discover the great city step by step, and soon came to know it even better than the locals, as she saw it with fresh eyes.

At the time she is writing this book, she is still comfortably living in Romania's capital, and although in her daily life she's a technical writer, she really loves blogging about her home country and the places she visits abroad.

Needless to say, Cristina enjoys traveling a lot, and discovering new cultures and the people that make them. Although she still enjoys Bucharest, with its many perks and hidden attractions, she dreams of one day moving to another country and starting a new journey.

Cristina Tărbuc

HOW TO USE THIS BOOK

This book was written by someone who has lived in an area for over three months. The author has made the best suggestions based on their own experiences in the area. Please check that these places are still available before traveling to the area. The goal of this book is to help travelers either dream or experience different locations by providing opinions from a local.

Cristina Tărbuc

FROM THE PUBLISHER

Traveling can be one of the most important moments in a person's life. The memories that you have of anticipating going somewhere new or getting to travel are some of the best. As a publisher of the Greater Than a Tourist book series, as well as the popular 50 Things to Know book series, we strive to help you learn about new places, spark your imagination, and inspire you.

Thought this book you will find something for every traveler. Wherever you are and whatever you do I wish you safe fun, and inspiring travel.

Lisa Rusczyk Ed. D.
CZYK Publishing

Cristina Tărbuc

WELCOME TO > TOURIST

Cristina Tărbuc

INTRODUCTION

Have you decided to come visit Bucharest? Congratulations, I can confirm you have made a great choice. Although not the most famous destination in the world, Bucharest might surprise you in a very pleasant way and leave you with the feeling you want to come back one day.

I moved to Bucharest in 2006, when I was 24, and this is basically where I started my adult life. There were many things I didn't like about it at first, such as the infernal traffic, the hot, dusty summers, some of the people (as with any capital, people are always in a rush, less caring about what goes on around them), the noise and the dirty streets (though you should not think that Bucharest generally is dirty, some areas are just less well kept than others), and finally, the beautiful old houses left in ruin.

In time, I learned to appreciated what it had to offer, like the wealth of work and study opportunities, the countless cultural events, the many doors open for you to become someone, the mixture of styles and places, the colorful pubs and cafes, the huge, green parks, and I could go on like this, but you will understand what I mean as you begin reading.

Don't be afraid to discover Bucharest, and don't come armed with judgment from the many advertisements warning to be cautious when visiting. You will discover that people are more open than you'd expect, you'll enjoy the city and the atmosphere. And I hope my advice will greatly contribute to your experience.

Cristina Tărbuc

1. Get to Town Safely from the Airport

If you are coming to Bucharest by plane, you will be landing on Otopeni Airport ("Aeroportul Internațional Henri Coandă"). While many people will rush to the machines to order a taxi (which is also a solution, as cabs in Bucharest are not expensive, provided you use one of the companies available in the airport taxi app), you can just exit on the usual path towards Arrivals, and then descend using the stairs to your right (look for signs pointing to the bus). There is an automatic vending machine, or you can purchase your ticket from the booth located exactly in the bus stop. The tickets to/from the airport (783 Express Bus, 24h/day) are more expensive than in-town trips, because you are actually travelling outside of Bucharest. A round-trip is less than 2 euro, so it's a very good alternative to taxies (which will cost around 7-8 euro or more, depending on where you want to go).

The 783 bus will get you as far as Piața Unirii, where you have connections with the Metro (Lines M1, M2, M3), other buses, taxis, etc. It also passes through popular places like Piața Victoriei, Piața Romana and University Square.

2. Rely on Public Transport

If you are staying in Bucharest for a week or even more, consider getting an Active RATB (public bus service) card, which can be charged with credit and used when needed, or charged with a subscription that allows you to have countless trips on the city's buses and trams (it costs around 10 euro/month).

You can look up the RATB website (also available in English) for information about tickets, subscriptions and useful tips. Once you have purchased and Active card, you can set up an online account and purchase your trips or subscriptions online.

The Bucharest metro is also a great way to get around, especially with a network as simple as Bucharest's. It uses a separate subscription, which is around 15 euro/month. The METROREX website (English version available) provides all the info you need, as well as a map of the underground lines.

3. Change your Money to Local Currency

If you are travelling from an EU country, you might think that you can pay in euro everywhere in Romania. You will soon find out that it is not the case. But fortunately, you can easily exchange your money into LEI (Romanian currency): exchange offices are located almost everywhere, from the airport lounge, to the streets of the city. As a general tip, you can try to find the best exchange rate by going to offices that are not located in the tourist areas. Also, banks and ATMS will charge you something for the exchange, so it might be good to avoid them.

There is one place that is famous for exchanging your money in the Old Center: Dristor Kebab (yes, it's a place selling *shawarma* and *kebap*) has one of the best rates, and it's open non-stop, so you can go there in confidence.

4. Dress According to the Season

With its temperate continental climate, Romania has all its four seasons in place. But they might be different from what you are used to back at home.

If you are visiting June to August, expect dry scorching heat and consider wearing a hat, sunscreen, light clothing and sun glasses. If you are visiting from December till February, you can expect just a few degrees Celsius over 0, but temperatures can often drop below 0, especially during the night. While it's not usual, sometimes we can have 15 degrees below zero, which is quite cold. With this in mind, come prepared with warm clothes, winter boots and jacket, gloves, hat and scarf. Of course, it all depends on where you're coming from. If you're used to cold weather, you'll be just fine.

The spring and autumn months are, in my opinion, the best times to visit. Consider planning your trip in April, May, or September for the best weather and scenery. Although it may be rainy (do pack a jacket and an umbrella), Bucharest is lovely in spring with its many blooming trees, while the colors of parks in autumn is amazing.

5. Buy an Antique Souvenir

Some like it vintage, and if that's your case, then you might wonder where in Bucharest you can buy a souvenir that's not kitsch, and that has a personality. I won't give you a full list of every antique shop in Bucharest, but I will make a few recommendations of places that are dear to me.

The first one is the former *Stock Exchange Palace* (*Strada Doamnei 11*), which now hosts a permanent exhibition of handmade and antique objects. If you go inside, you might find yourself captivated by the many old objects for sale or the colorful handmade jewelry and decorative objects.

Also in the Old Center area you have *Thomas Antiques*, a place you can easily spend some time in, considering it looks like a museum, and also has a bar!

And one of my personal favorites, a small shop in the Cotroceni area, called *Cotroceni Vintage House*, sells old furniture and decorations, but is also a small bistro.

Whichever you chose, you should know that antique shops in Bucharest are not the cheapest places to buy gifts. However, they might be worth it.

6. Find the Best Gifts to Bring Back Home

If you are the gift-giving type, I'm sure you're always thinking of what you might bring back to friends and family from your trips. And with Bucharest, this can be a tricky task. But here are some suggestions that could help you:

Local ceramic/pottery. You can find small ceramic items with traditional patterns in any souvenir shop, but they're cheaper in supermarkets (try Cora or Auchan's special area with traditional items).

Branded alcoholic drinks. In any gift shop or supermarket, you will easily spot the special *țuică* or *palincă* bottles, which can make for a great gift.

Traditional *ie* blouses (original or not). While authentic traditional blouses can cost 100 euro or more, you can settle for a commercial version made from quality linen for which you will pay around 20 euro. You can find them in many no-name shops around town, just look for them in the shop windows.

Bonus, the gift shop at the Village Museum ("Muzeul Satului") has a lot of cool stuff you can bring home to your loved ones, and it's also quality stuff, so you can buy in confidence.

7. Visit a Mall or Two

For all the *fashionistas* out there, but not only, Bucharest has a huge array of shopping malls, placed strategically around the city. Of these, the most appreciated are *Afi Cotroceni*, *Băneasa Shopping City*, *Unirea Shopping Center*, and *Vitan Mall*. Although not as cheap as in other countries, brand stores in Bucharest often have good discounts and locals will rush in to get a good deal. If you want to mingle and feel at home, join us for a shopping spree in one of the many malls, and wrap it up with ice-cream or a visit to the cinema.

8. Enjoy a 3D Cinema Experience

Since 3D cinema came to Bucharest, it has almost become the standard for cinema lovers. In other words, if we're going out to see a movie, it had better be a 3D movie!

There are many 3D cinemas around Bucharest, but the one that's most advertised (and most expensive) is the T IMAX cinema in *Afi Cotroceni* mall, because of the shape of its screen, that supposedly accounts for a more immersive experience.

A cheaper variant would be *Cinema Pro* in the old center. This one's particularly advantageous because it lack the crowds and lets you enjoy a more intimate experience.

9. Shop for Books in the Coolest Places

The bookstore trend has always been big in Bucharest, but now it's taking a whole new dimension. Bookshops are becoming more than places to buy books, and you can see that for yourselves if you head to one of the *Cărturești* bookshops, which are also places where you can enjoy a cup of tea, attend an exhibition or a book launch and listen to tranquil music. And they don't just sell books. I usually spend one or two hours just browsing through their accessories for coffee and tea making, cook books, packs of tea and specialty chocolate, decorative objects, gadgets and funny gift ideas.

Their largest shop, *Cărturești Carusel* (Lipscani 55), is worth visiting if only for the architecture and setup. The elegant 19th century building went through a lot before becoming the beautiful bookstore it is today. There are six levels (1000 sq m) in total, including a bistro on the last floor, a multimedia space in the basement and a gallery for contemporary art on the first floor. Another bookstore I really like is *Antic Exlibris* (*Strada Doamnei 23*). As the name suggests, it's a store that sells old books, or more precisely, books from old collections. Most books are in English, and the shop also sells toys, DIY sets, creative stationery items, the kind you won't find in a common bookstore.

10. Have a Cup of (Ice) Tea

Whether it's cold and snowy, rainy or fair, you can always enjoy a cup of tea or coffee in one of Bucharest's quiet tea houses and cafes. They come in all shapes and sizes, from the ones with a *shabby chic* design, such as *Caffe D'Arthe* or *Santhe Fitoceainarie* (a social cafe, where everything costs 8 lei and you can pay in advance for a poor person's meal from the menu options), to the more quirky or themed ones, such as *Ramayana Cafe* (Indian theme), *Voila Bistrot* (French-themed bistro with a bohemian/artistic feel), *Ceainaria Cinci* (colorful, bohemian design), *Acuarela* (nostalgic childhood theme), or *Infinitea* (interwar decor).

Cristina Tărbuc

There is no such place as Budapest.
Perhaps you are thinking of Bucharest,
and there is no such place as Bucharest,
either. (Robert Benchley)

Cristina Tărbuc

11. Try the Traditional Food

There's not much we can call our own when talking about Romanian food and drinks. There are no special ingredients growing on our lands, that no other country has ever seen before, so don't expect anything too exotic or unheard of. Instead, you can rely on Romanians for hearty, rich meals that can easily be considered comfort food, and recipes you can always take home with you. Romanian "cuisine", if you can call it such, has borrowed and adapted from the neighboring countries. That's why most of our prized local recipes and foods are also considered traditional in Hungary, Turkey, Russia, or Moldova, of course, under different names. Which doesn't make them less tasty or addictive.

Some of the most well-known "traditional Romanian" dishes you will be able to try while in Bucharest are: *sarmale*, local cheeses and cured meats, traditional spreads (*zacuscă, salată de vinete*), delicious stews (*tochitură, tocană, gulaș, ciulama*), and, of course, our famed traditional sour soups (*ciorbă de burtă, ciorbă de fasole, ciorbă de perișoare*).

Where to get them? You can try any of the following traditional restaurants: La Copac (*Pitar Moș 23*); Hanu' lui Manuc (*Franceză 62-64*); La Mama (*Episcopiei 9 / Splaiul Independenței 210-213 / Str. Băcani 1*); Taverna Covaci (*Covaci 1*); Lacrimi și Sfinți (*Șepcari 16*); Caru cu Bere (*Stavropoleos 5*).

12. Hunt Down your Fresh Food

Some visitors like to rent out apartments and live like locals, cooking for themselves. It's also cheaper than a hotel, so it's a win-win. And if you want to cook your own meals, you might want to know where to find the best ingredients.

Bucharest has a supermarket or two in every neighborhood, so finding food should not be a problem. However, if you want to enjoy the local experience, find the neighborhood market. Regardless of where you're staying, there likely is one within walking distance.

What to buy there? Well, fresh fruit and vegetables for one. But don't hurry to the tables with shiny looking produce, the local producers are usually placed at the sides and exits, and not in the best spots. Then, there's cheese and cured meats. For these, it's best to look for separate kiosks on which the words *Sibiu*, or *sibieni* are displayed. They sell quality dairy products, all sorts of cured meats, and sometimes free range eggs.

Almost every market has butcher shops, where you can find quality meat (not always though, so use your best judgment when buying). This is also where you can find a fishmonger's shop, if you're the kind of person who loves fish.

Other than that, at the market you will find all sorts of knick-knacks, such as cleaning products, plumbing supplies, clothing items, etc.

13. Shop in Bucharest's Largest Marketplace

Bucur Obor market has been around until the 18th century, and is the largest market in town. Built on the place of Bucharest's old gallows, *Halele Obor* are now a huge complex of stands where you can buy literally anything, from fresh greens to meat and clothes. Near the market, *Bucur Obor shop* is an old department store that somehow managed to keep a communist look and feel. It is actually a collection of individual shops, selling clothing, pottery, jewelry, cosmetics, articles for the house, literally anything. However, it's mainly known for the shops selling textiles, leather and accessories for sewing (if you're a handmade artist, it's here that you can find cheaper materials, for example).

14. Have a Cup of Mulled Wine at the Christmas Market

Every year at the end of November, the Bucharest Christmas Market opens in one of Bucharest's central areas. In 2016, the location was Piața Constituției, while in previous years, it was held at Piața Universității. You can enjoy a cup of mulled wine or hot chocolate, check out the beautiful Christmas decorations (some made by artisans), traditional masks, winter clothes and accessories, handmade jewelry, religious icons, traditional weaves, and buy great delicacies, from home made sweets to cured meats and cheese. Music concerts are also scheduled as part of the Christmas market.

15. Enjoy your Winter on Skates

As I mentioned before, Bucharest has all its four seasons well defined. And winter time is when the skating rinks start to open. While at Liberty Mall, Mall Grand Arena and Afi Palace Cotroceni mall skating rinks are open all year, the ones in Cişmigiu, Alexandru Ioan Cuza, Herăstrău, Tineretului and Drumul Taberei parks are only open in winter. If you want to feel the holiday spirit, these might just be the places to start from, especially since other attractions can also be found in these parks.

16. Find the Festival for You

As soon as the warm season is in, Bucharest prepares for a series of fairs and festivals, that can take place literally anywhere, from parks to the streets of the Old Center, and from the front yard of a pub to the city's main exhibition locations. There are vintage fairs, yard sales, food festivals of all sorts, book fairs, cultural events, animal shows, car shows, and I could go on forever.

Whenever I want to see what's cooking, I look at the events nearby on Facebook, and I kid you not, there is always something happening somewhere in Bucharest.

Of course, some events are free, and some (like music festivals or exhibits) are not. Make sure you pick yours wisely, based on your own preferences.

To give you just an idea, here are some local events from the summer of 2017 (most of which are recurring): Bucharest Jazz Festival, ShortsUP (short films festival), Rock the City, George Enescu classical music festival, Living statues festival, BurgerFest, Street Delivery (urban manifesto for architecture and arts), Pet Expo, Astrofest, Spotlight (Bucharest International Light Festival). And of course, there are a lot of season-related events, such as Christmas and Easter festivals.

So don't be surprised to run into an event happening during your visit in Bucharest.

17. Plan for the Perfect Concert

As in any capital city, every year there are many concerts scheduled to take place in Bucharest. Some may be of worldwide known artists, and some may be of local artists, so if you enjoy listening to live music, you might want to check the concert agenda before you come visit.

For big names concerts, you can check out the *eventful.com* website, which provides information about the more visible events in Bucharest. For local artists or smaller concerts, you can check out the music events section of Facebook for Bucharest, or the events page of individual places that usually have live music (for example, *Fabrica* or *Berăria H* are some of the places that host concerts on a regular basis).

18. Visit an Indoor Museum

As any big city, Bucharest has many museums, and a visit to one of them can be a great activity, especially on cold or rainy days. The *Palace of Parliament* or *Cotroceni Palace* are the ones best known to visitors, but there are many others worth seeing.

My personal favorites are Grigore Antipa Museum of Natural History, Muzeul Țăranului (Peasant's Museum) and Dimitrie Leonida Technical Museum.

The true romantics (and not only) could be interested in the astronomic observation sessions held at Casa Filipescu-Cesianu.

19. Get a Glimpse of Tradition at the Village Museum

The Village Museum of Bucharest, a collection of buildings recreating rural life between the 17th & 20th centuries, is more than a museum, it feels as a real walk in a Romanian village.

Inside its walls you will see how our grandparents lived some years ago (some of them still do), you will admire the outsides and insides of homes from all over Romania, as well as old wooden churches, wind, water mills and other installations, wells, a sheep cot, a smithery, and even a former inn, which now is open as a restaurant with traditional Romanian food.

The Village Museum often hosts tradition-related events, where craftsmen and food producers sell quality products, such as honey, cheese, cakes, sausages, traditional costumes, masks, various weaves (same as the ones you see inside the museum houses), painted icons and other handcrafted objects. In my opinion, it's your best chance to get a quality souvenir from Romania, as most souvenir shops sell unauthentic objects (usually at high prices too).

At the entrance, next to where you buy your tickets (around 2 euro) you can visit the museum shop, which sells authentic traditional pottery, weaves and clothing, but also fridge magnets and other less traditional souvenirs.

My advice is to visit the Village Museum if you get to Bucharest, it's the closest you'll get to Romanian traditions in a big city. Besides, since the museum is practically a park, it's also a great relaxation place.

20. Shop for Art Supplies

Are you an artist, or do you simply enjoy doing something creative from time to time? In the Old Center, between Lipscani and Blănari streets, there's a small road bordered by art supply shops and art galleries. It's no Montmartre, but it's as close as it gets. This colorful street is called *Hanul cu Tei* and at its end is a restaurant with the same name. In summer, the space gets crowded with tables from the restaurant, but for the rest of the year, it's one of the most charming places in Bucharest.

Cristina Tărbuc

I came to Bucharest two years ago with a legion of conquering heroes. I leave with a troupe of gigolos and racketeers! (German Field Marshal August von Mackensen, on the moral effects of the German occupation of Bucharest during the World War I)

Cristina Tărbuc

21. Listen (and Dance) to Traditional Music

There are a few places in the Old Center that have live traditional music, and sometimes even dances.

One of them is *Caru' cu bere* (*Str. Stavropoleos 5*), where there is a live dance show every evening around 8 PM. Don't forget to book a table, the place is usually crowded and you might not get in to see it.

Another is *Hanu' lui Manuc* (*Str. Franceză 62-64*), that has traditional *taraf* music every evening, most of the time followed by dances.

22. Hit the Clubs like you Mean it

I must admit I'm not the usual club client, but many of my foreign friends have confessed they come to Bucharest for the night life, so there must be something to it. The Old Center is abundant with clubs, and if you walk up Șelari street, you will be overwhelmed by the loud music, the entertainers dancing in the windows, and the shiny lights.

As far as tastes go, Bucharest has all kinds of clubs: house music, rock music, rock'n roll, Latin or dance, there's something for everyone. Some clubs target students and younger people in general, others are for a more bling-crazed, fashion-sworn public, there are specialized rock clubs known only to the people of the house or hipster clubs in unconventional places. Whether you stumble in a club with a vintage feel, a bouncy fast-paced place, or an eccentric sugar daddy's heaven, in Bucharest you have it all. Either do your research in advance, let your Romanian friends choose for your, or just try your luck. You'll probably end up having heaps of fun even if you don't end up where you planned.

23. Head Down to the ... Beach?

No, there is no actual natural beach in Bucharest, but that doesn't mean you can't enjoy a day in the sun with cool waves around you. There are several public pools where you can get your perfect sun tan, for access prices around 10 - 15 euro / day.

In summer, locals trying to get away from the heat of the city will either head to the seaside, or settle for a cheaper substitute, like one of the city's swimming pools, such as *Player Pool*, *Piscina Floreasca*, *Bamboo*, or *Daimon Pool*.

But the exciting news is that, on the 1st of July 2017, *Therme București* opened the largest urban beach in Europe (*Sands of Therme*), with a surface of 30,000 square meters and a setup reminding of tropical beaches. Is that cool or what?

Therme București is a huge complex that has everything from outdoor and indoor pools, jacuzzi, restaurant, sauna, cocktail bar, acquatic playground, hydro-massage, spa treatments and more.

It can be reached by free transport, from Piața Romană.

24. Enjoy a View from Above

Have you ever wondered how Bucharest looks from up high? Well, you can try and see for yourself.

Join the tour for the Palace of Parliament and see the grand view that Ceauşescu saw when he was president. The tour will take you to a balcony that offers a full view of Bulevardul Unirii, a street that was specially created to fit in a grand plan (actually, the axis of the city was modified in order to create this boulevard stretching from the Palace and all the way down to Piața Alba Iulia).

Other great belvedere spots, offering views over different areas, are some of the city's sky bars, such as *Sole* restaurant (*Bd. Iancu de Hunedoara 48*), *18 Lounge* (*Piața Presei Libere 3-5, City Gate, South Tower*), *Club InterContinental Lounge* (*Bulevardul Nicolae Bălcescu 4*), or *Upstairs Rooftop* (*Sevastopol 24*).

25. Try an Escape Room Experience

You've probably already heard of, or even tried an escape room experience. If you've never heard of it, it's an activity that combines problem-solving with team work and can make for a great team building activity. Basically, your team is up against the clock trying to escape a place by finding clues and solving puzzles, with the purpose of getting out as fast as possible.

The concept may be old (in the past, there used to be quite a few TV shows based on it), but now there's a real trend in Bucharest, and you can chose from several escape rooms, each with their own twist.

In case you're visiting with a group, or planning to meet with a few Romanian friends during your stay in Bucharest, this could be your opportunity to plan for a great activity, especially if you're into logic and problem-solving.

26. Have Fun at Board Game Night

Board games have been a huge hit in the past few years, and places for game lovers quickly started appearing.

Whether your Romanian friends have asked you to join a game at their place, or you are meeting up in a place like *Epic Bar* (*Colţei 50*), *Lente* (*Dionisie Lupu 78*), *Ludic* (*Aaron Florian 3A*), or *Journey Pub* (*George Enescu 25*), you might as well enjoy a night of board gaming like the locals do.

27. Have a Beer ... or 100

A few years ago, we only had some bland local beers and beer itself was seen as an inferior beverage. But fortunately, this has greatly changed, and now we have more and more local producers of specialty beers, competing with the huge variety of imported beers found in supermarkets and pubs.

If you appreciate beer the same way a true wine lover thinks of wine, then here's where you get the most variety.

Auchan has by far the best selection of beers from all the supermarkets. If you want to take your time selecting the perfect beer for home, that's where you should go.

In the Old Center, two pubs are fighting a battle of who has the biggest beer selection. The first one is called, no surprise here, *100 de beri* (translates as *100 beers*) and you can find it at *no. 8 Covaci* street. The other is *Beer O'Clock*, at *no. 4 Gabroveni* street. Other pubs with a varied beer menu are *Explorer's* (*Strada Franceză 46-48*) and *Nenea Iancu* (*Strada Covaci 3*).

Care to try out Romanian beer? Have a go at some local brands such as: Silva (blonde, dark), Zăganu (blonde, red, dark or IPA), Terapia or Morning Glory.

28. Try Out the Best Burgers

Yes, burger culture has also hit Bucharest, and we are glad it did, because we took it to the next level.

With many hip places now including burgers in their menus, there is competition, and this means everyone tries to deliver the best burger. And that's great, because instead of industrial ingredients you are likely to get handmade buns and sauces, fresh veggies, and "real potato" fries instead of frozen ones.

Some great places for burgers (and pub food generally) in Bucharest are: *Vivo Food Bar* (*Calea Floreasca 60*), *Modelier* (*Strada Duzilor 12*), *Lokal* (*Mihai Eminescu 57*), *Switch.Eat* (*Strada Horei 34*) and *Copper's Pub* (*Bulevardul Hristo Botev 25*).

29. Get Lost in the Urban Jungle

Big towns are great, but sometimes we just want to step out of the noise and agitation and find a place to enjoy a lemonade in the middle of nature. And in Bucharest, you can easily enjoy your drinks in the cozy space of one of the many summer gardens spread around the city. But there aren't many who can earn the title of *jungles*. In fact, I will only tell you about two:

Grădina Eden is excellently located, right behind Ştirbey Palace, not far from Cişmigiu Park or the Romanian Athenaeum. It stretches on a large space where you can literally get lost, as the rich vegetation hides and unveils several tables and chairs and the bars where you can buy alcoholic drinks or fancy fresh juice and specialty lemonades. With its bohemian look and feel, it's one of those place where you can forget about everything and just chill.

In a different part of the city, *Piranha* is a different kind of special. This restaurant actually makes sense of the expression "urban jungle", as you will be enjoying your food and drinks in the middle of a real natural reservation. The artificial pond is filled with fish, and there are birds hanging around in the specially arranged cages. And don't be surprised if a peacock joins you for dinner every now and then, as they often walk around freely. The rich vegetation and the wooden decor completes the jungle look. Although it might not be famous for its food, this place is definitely special and worth a visit.

30. Wake up and Smell the Coffee

I think any coffee lover will agree that there's nothing quite like the fresh smell of coffee in the morning. In Bucharest, *Delicatese Florescu* is the go to place for good coffee. It sells gourmet coffee roasted after old original Armenian recipes handed down to the current owner by Avedis Carabelaian, an Armenian who is known as one of Bucharest's legendary coffee merchants from the WWII period.

The tiny coffee shop on *Str. Radu Cristian 6* could go unnoticed, if it wasn't from the insane roasted coffee smell coming from inside as you pass by. You can buy the beans and grind them yourself at home, or ask the shop assistant to do it for you. Most people will buy coffee from the *Carabelaian* range, but several rare and more expensive brands are also found here. The shop also has an online presence, for those who want to order home, or decide on what to buy before actually getting there. And you can also enjoy a strong coffee on the spot, prepared as in the old times.

Besides coffee, at *Delicatese Florescu* you can buy tea, sweets, drinks, all kinds of delicacies, as well as small gifts and coffee-making utensils.

Cristina Tărbuc

Bucharest possesses truly one of the more unique urban environments of any European capital city. Beautiful interbellic architecture is in a state of spectacular decay and laid on top of this erratically are various aspects of the 21st century. (Paul Wood)

Cristina Tărbuc

31. Discover a Hidden 19th Century Monastery

You may have heard of Stavropoleos monastery, but that's not the only old monastery in Bucharest. In the Piața Romană area, not far from Grădina Icoanei park, well hidden behind a white wall, is *Schitul Dârvari*, a building from 1834, that is currently home to a small community of monks. The small church and beautiful, neat garden breathe tranquility and modesty, even if they are hidden in one of the most lively areas of the city.

Address: Strada Schitul Dârvari 3

32. Get Lost in an Experimental Neighborhood

Between 1955 and 1957, the communist leadership decided to build post-calamity collective housing for people who had been moved around because of the war, most of whom came from Bessarabia. These houses were built following a special architecture, their most interesting feature being a common porch which can be accessed from the street through an archway. There are six streets in total, called Întrecerii, Năzuinței, Prieteniei, Cutezătorilor, Doicești and Fildeșului, and the houses here are like nowhere else in Bucharest. Their residents still live like a closed, private community, knowing and helping each other much like in a village rather than the city.

So why come here? To see an unique spot in the city, completely broken from the rest of the world (it's said that here even the dogs' barks are whispered).

How to get to Cățelu?

By metro: get off at either Piața Muncii or Dristor station and walk about 10 minutes

By tram: take tram no. 1 to Baba Novac station

By bus: buses 311, 70 and 79 also stop at Baba Novac station

33. Go on a Tour of Communist Relics

While Bucharest's most famous building is undoubtedly the Palace of Parliament, there is a whole tour you can embark on to discover the traces of communism.

You can start at the fountains on Bulevardul Unirii, and walk between the Palace of Parliament with the complex of buildings around it, the former Bragadiru beer factory and Bragadiru Palace, and Carol Park with the Monument of the Heroes. While it's not the prettiest area of Bucharest, you will not be unsafe, and you will get to see the real Bucharest, as well as a glimpse of old Bucharest.

34. Walk around Piața Romană

Go on a walk starting from the *Universitate* metro station (University Square), taking a detour on the lovely streets around *Grădina Icoanei* park, exiting into *Mihai Eminescu* street to get to the *Academy of Economic Studies*, then going for a spin around *Piața Amzei*, with its many hidden treasures.

There are no huge touristic objectives to be seen, but I promise you will find a lot of intriguing places and especially a lot of cozy and well hidden restaurants and pubs you will love. And if you take this trip in spring, you will be amazed of the streets with beautiful old houses and wonderful gardens, the street art and the colorful scenery all around (though winter also has its charm at *Piața Romană*).

Some of the things to check out on this walk: the statues in front of the National Theater, the Italian Catholic Church, Café Verona (beautiful summer terace), the Anglican Chuch, Ioanid (Ion Voicu) Park, Shift Pub, Piua Book Bar.

35. Visit a Former Communist Prison

The communist period has really left a mark on Romania, influencing our personalities, perhaps not in the best way. But it is part of our history and we must acknowledge it in order to be free from it.

Perhaps the saddest part of it was the imprisonment, torture and killing of many intellectuals, and practically anyone who was against the system.

Not far from Bucharest *Fortul 13, Jilava* (known as a real *Romanian Auschwitz*) is now a memorial museum open to visitors. Visits must be programmed in advance through a dedicated website, and every visitor must bring along an ID, to be left at the gate all through the visit. You cannot use your phones, but are encouraged to bring a camera, take pictures and spread the word about the place.

To get there, you have a special bus (no. 425) from the station *CFR Progresul* (reachable by trams 4, 7 and 25) going to the station *Bumbăcăria Jilava* in Jilava village. From there, you can easily walk to the former prison.

36. Discover a Lovely 18th Century Palace

Mogoşoaia Palace and the domain surrounding it has become a favorite destination not only for relaxation, but also for beautiful weddings and other events. And it should be no surprise, as the natural setting is amazing, and the palace's architecture perfectly reflects the *Brâncovenesc* style specific to Romania.

The complex includes the Palace built by Constantin Brâncoveanu, the princely kitchen, a 19th century chapel, the Mogoşoaia greenhouses, a 18th century church and a former ice cellar.

The rose gardens, the green bushes somewhat reminiscent of Versailles, the lake view, the beautiful park around the complex make it a destination to remember.

You can reach it by taking the bus no. 460 from Parc Bazilescu all the way to Mogoşoaia.

37. Find the Delta in the Middle of the City

How would you feel about stumbling on a real delta in the middle of the city? Covering 183 hectares, the *Văcărești Nature Park* is a wetland formed on the site of a hydro-technical project started in 1986 and left unfinished. The area is 4 km away from the city center, not far from a residential complex. It was declared a protected area in 2016, as it had become home to several species of water birds, as well as muskrats, foxes, weasels, reptiles, amphibians, invertebrates, and perhaps best of all, otters.

An observatory has been set up in the Asmita Gardens residential complex, offering visitors a panoramic view of the park.

If you would like to get there, consider talking to a local to help you set up a visit, or access the park's official website and use their contact form.

38. Go for a Stroll in the Park

There are quite a few parks and lakes in Bucharest, and each seems to have its own personality and energy. While the most famous is Herăstrău, you will not be disappointed by Cişmigiu (a park with history), Tineretului, Carol or Titan parks. Build around large lakes, these parks can be great recreation places and are often full of people enjoying their walks, bike rides, coffee or food. You can rent bikes or boats or enjoy a fresh drink at one of the many cafes, and sometimes even visit a museum within the area.

Parks are also the preferred location for a number of events, so don't be surprised if you happen to stumble on a living statues event, an open air concert, a food festival or a sports competition while going for a walk in the park.

39. Pedal Away from Park to Park

Do you enjoy getting around by bike? Even if you didn't bring your own, you can rent a bike and use it to discover the city.
In Herăstrău park (Charles de Gaulle entrance) and Tineretului park (Gheorghe Șincai entrance), you will notice some yellow city bikes waiting for you. They have *i'velo* written on them and you can rent them for 1 to 24 hours (don't forget to bring an ID with you). One hour costs 5 lei, and you will pay only 20 lei for 24h. Just don't forget to bring them back in good shape!

40. Go Hiking in the Forest

On occasions such as Easter or Labor Day, we love to get away to a green place and relax. One of the closest places from Bucharest where you can enjoy a nice day out is the *Comana Natural Park*, a protected area which can be easily reached from the city.

Part of the park, the *Neajlov Delta* (or *Comana Moor*) is the largest wetland in the South of Romania and a preferred nesting place for a large number of birds, which attracts many bird watching enthusiasts.

Comana Park is a great place for hiking and enjoying nature. Don't forget to pack some food for a nice picnic during your hike.

You can get to the park by taking one of the hourly minibuses leaving to Comana from the pickup points at Eroii Revoluției (Pieptănari) and CFR Progresul (the end station of tram no. 25). The trip takes 50-60 minutes.

Cristina Tărbuc

I was born near Bucharest, but my parents came to France a year later. We moved back to Romania when I was thirteen, and my world was shattered. I hated Bucharest, its society, and its mores - its anti-Semitism for example. (Eugene Ionesco)

Cristina Tărbuc

41. Find the Most Colorful Temple in Town

The *Coral* temple in Bucharest was designed after the Leopoldstadt temple in Viena, and is one the most colorful and interesting buildings in town. It was built in 1866 in neo-Moorish style, and its richly decorated interior is a feast for the eyes.

Find it hidden in plain sight at *Sfânta Vineri 9*, in the Old Center of Bucharest.

42. Enjoy a Day around Animals for Free

A while back, I discovered this incredibly nice animal shelter which you can reach even without a car, if you are willing to walk about 20 minutes from the tram station. *Steaua Speranței* is a shelter for abandoned horses, although it also has 2 llamas, several dogs, chickens and ponies. It is a happy, colorful place, great for children and adults alike. You can reach it by taking the tram no. 21 from Piața Sf. Gheorghe (center area). You must get off at the 9th stop, then continue walking on the right side of the road until you reach a small plant shop. You will see the signs pointing to a ranch, and that's where you must turn right. The guard at the shelter will ask for your name and signature before you can visit the place. You can stay as long as you want, and you can bring carrots to feed the horses, or make a small donation, if you wish.

43. Have a Picnic or a Barbeque

With so many green spaces around, going on a picnic can be a great activity. Of course, it can be as fancy as planning a full meal, or just packing a couple of sandwiches and a good book, and heading to a nice spot in a park. If any of that sounds good to you, then consider one of the following locations:

In *Herăstrău* park, on Rose Island, there are a few great spots by the water, under the willow trees. The setting is almost magical.

Alexandru Ioan Cuza park also has several spots where you can set up your blanket on the grass and enjoy a picnic. I prefer the spots that are near the edges of the lake.

The green spaces around *Mogoşoaia Palace* are another great choice for picnic and relaxation lovers.

But if you really want to go local, consider passing to the last level: have a barbeque outside. Romanians really love their barbecues and this reflects in the special spaces with grills you can find in several public places:

At the back of *Crângaşi* park, there are 7 pavilions set up with grills for barbequing.

In *Parcul Lumea Copiilor*, you can rent a grill with your ID card. But the most spectacular place to have a barbeque is at *Mogoşoaia Palace*. In a less crowded day, you can enjoy a real feast in a place of amazing natural beauty.

44. Find an Amusement Park

Now, everyone has their own definition of amusement, but we can all agree an amusement park can be a fun way to spend time. Here are some suggestions in Bucharest and surrounding areas:

Parc de Agrement Tei (*Chiristigiilor nr. 11-13, Bucharest*) is a fun park with a special theme: characters from Romanian fairy tales. Its main attractions are the rollercoaster and the big wheel.

Water Park (*Calea Bucureştilor 255, Otopeni*) can be reached by taking buses 783,780 or 449 to the station ICSITMUA. As suggested by the name, it's a water games and sports park.

Divertiland (*Divertismentului nr. 1, Autostrada Bucureşti-Piteşti*) is another water park with heaps of fun activities. You can get there by taking their special bus from *Preciziei* metro station, or by taking buses 137 or 236 all the way to the *Kika-Hornbach* station.

Parc Aventura Comana (*Gellu Naum 607, Comana, Giurgiu*) is 35 km from Bucharest and can be reached by taking the minibus from a pickup point at Eroii Revoluţiei (Pieptănari). Set up in a beautiful natural area, the park is great for climbing, boating, or crossing the lake by Tyrolean traverse.

A great place, especially for kids, is the Animal Farm (*Ferma Animalelor, Sfântul Gheorghe 20, Pantelimon*), which can be reached by taking a minibus no. 547 from Obor / Pantelimon. This is a petting zoo where kids can learn more about farm animals and enjoy various organized activities.

45. Visit an Artificial Island on an Artificial Lake

Lacul Morii is the largest lake in Bucharest, covering 246 hectares. This artificial lake and the island in its middle have a short, but interesting story. The lake was built in 1986, on the location of a former cemetery and church. To build it, 12,000 graves were moved and the church was demolished, along with about 400 houses (the residents were given collective lodgings instead). The former space was covered in concrete, and water filled in the newly created basin. The island that now looks like an abandoned ghost place was supposed to be a great recreational space. Now, there is only a pavilion, a decorative well, a pier and a lot of garbage.

Photography enthusiasts are especially drawn to this place, as it has real photogenic potential.

All around the lake, there is a path which is ideal for riding your bike. In the evening, many locals go running on the same path. This is also the place where aviation shows are sometimes organized.

How to reach *Lacul Morii* and its island? Take the metro or the tram no. 41 to *Crângaşi* station.

46. Find the Only Street in Steps

From *Carol I* park, cross the street opposite the entrance to the park, then go left on Constantin Istrati street. Immediately, you will run into a stairway that is painted with different scenes. This is actually a tiny street called *Xenofon*, the only one made of steps in Bucharest. The painting (that changes from time to time) was part of a project started in 2014, which aimed to make certain small streets known to the people.

If you climb the steps all the way up, you will arrive at Carol Park Hotel, considered by some the most luxurious hotel in Romania. Here, you will be on the highest natural point in Bucharest. Behind Carol Park Hotel, you will quickly recognize the Palace of Parliament building in the distance.

47. Discover a Secret Stairway

A visit to the Patriarchal Palace up on the Metropolitan Hill is also an opportunity to discover a secret stairway.

Right before the belfry, on your left, between two old houses (the one on the left has a beautiful wooden porch), you will notice some stairs made of stone, that seem to disappear behind the buildings. The stair takes you down to a street called Ienăchiţă Văcărescu, in an area that used to be known as the *Flămânda* suburb or outskirts (in the 18th century, this was a poor suburb, its name meaning literally *the hungry one*).

While descending the stairs, look around you and check out all the cool details and signs. You can continue to discover the street below, and then return the same way, or even wonder further (don't forget to have a map with you).

48. Meet a Local or Two

Many people, including myself, like to get in touch with locals when in another country. In Bucharest, you have a number of ways to do this. You might sign onto a website such as Couchsurfing or Meetup, and reach out to people directly or join a meeting. Or you might prefer to approach people in a bar or a pub. If you're the easygoing type, you'll have no problem starting a casual conversation with someone, as Bucharest's youth is nowadays more relaxed and very friendly towards newcomers. You will notice many of us speak good English, have a healthy sense of humor and enough knowledge of the outside world to make for enjoyable companions.

And depending on your age and interests, you will most likely end up making friends at the events and places you're attending.

49. Learn Some Romanian Phrases

Romanian is not an easy languages, considering it has so many rules, and even more exceptions to the rules. But if you want to see the joy in the eyes of your new Romanian friends, try learning some simple common phrases, such as *Noroc!* [no-rok] (Cheers!), *Salut!* [Sa-lut] (Hi/Hello!), *Mulţumesc!* [Mool-tsoo-mesk] (Thanks!), *Bună dimineaţa!* [Boo-nuh di-mi-na-tsa] (Good morning!), *Bună ziua!* [Boo-nuh zee-wa] (Hi! - said during the day), *Bună seara!* [Boo-nuh sea-ra] (Good evening!), or *La revedere!* [La rev-eh-de-ray] (Good bye!).

50. Plan a Train Trip to the Mountains

So you've picked Bucharest for your holiday destination, and you're staying for more than a weekend, so you are probably considering getting out of the capital and discovering other places. The good news is that from Bucharest you can pick a number of nice destinations in Romania, easy to reach even without a personal car. E.g., from *Gara de Nord* train station, there are trains that can take you to several interesting locations, of which the most sought by tourists (and closest) are the mountain resorts in the *Valea Prahovei* area (Sinaia, Azuga, Bușteni, Predeal, etc.).

Of these, Sinaia, is the closest to Bucharest and the one with the most potential, both from a cultural point of view and as a starting point for mountain hiking courses.

To get there by train: Access the CFR website, select your travel date, enter *București Nord* as your departure point and *Sinaia* as the arrival point, then click Search. You will get a list of available trains.

It's possible to buy tickets online and print them in advance if you create an account on the *CFR Călători* website (for that, go to Login after you have initiated the search for your train). You get a 5% discount for buying online, and another 5% if you check the return ticket box. Other discounts apply if you purchase your tickets in advance, or if you are traveling with a group.

Cristina Tărbuc

Top Reasons to Book This Trip

- Vibrant urban life: Clubs, pubs, summer gardens and events at every corner.
- People: Friendly locals, always keen to meet you.
- Food: Simple, traditional comfort food.
- Nature: Beautiful parks, easy trips to the mountains and seaside.

Cristina Tărbuc

> TOURIST

GREATER THAN A TOURIST

Visit GreaterThanATourist.com
http://GreaterThanATourist.com

Sign up for the Greater Than a Tourist
Newsletter
http://eepurl.com/cxspyf

Follow us on Facebook:
https://www.facebook.com/GreaterThanATourist

Follow us on Pinterest:
http://pinterest.com/GreaterThanATourist

Follow us on Instagram:
http://Instagram.com/GreaterThanATourist

Cristina Tărbuc

> TOURIST

GREATER THAN A TOURIST

Please leave your honest review of this book on Amazon and Goodreads. Thank you.

We appreciate your positive and negative feedback as we try to provide tourist guidance in their next trip from a local.

> TOURIST

GREATER THAN A TOURIST

You can find Greater Than a Tourist books on Amazon.

Cristina Tărbuc

> TOURIST

GREATER THAN A TOURIST

WHERE WILL YOU TRAVEL TO NEXT?

Cristina Tărbuc

> TOURIST

GREATER THAN A TOURIST

Our Story

Traveling is a passion of this series creator. She studied abroad in college, and for their honeymoon Lisa and her husband toured Europe. During her travels to Malta, an older man tried to give her some advice based on his own experience living on the island since he was a young boy. She thought he was just trying to sell her something. When traveling to some places she was wary to talk to locals because she was afraid that they weren't being genuine. She created this book series to give you as a tourist an inside view on the place you are exploring and the ability to learn what locals would like to tell tourist. A topic that they are very passionate about.

Cristina Tărbuc

> TOURIST

GREATER THAN A TOURIST

Notes

Printed in Poland
by Amazon Fulfillment
Poland Sp. z o.o., Wrocław

34106244R00059